contents

British & North American Readers
Please note that Australian cup and spoon
measurements are metric. A quick conversion
guide appears on page 63.

the perfect roast

Roasts are a relatively simple affair, but a few shared

- Remove any silver sinew from beef fillet to prevent shrinkage and toughening.
- Select a baking dish large enough to fit the roast; make sure the meat does not extend over the sides.
- A rack in a baking dish helps good circulation of heat around the meat.
- The meat should have reached room temperature before cooking.
- When tying a roast, wet the kitchen string first. As the string dries (from the heat of the oven) it will shrink, holding the meat firm.
- Before heating the oven, check that the oven racks are in position.
- Meat can be cooked in an oven bag to prevent spatter and retain moisture; however, roasting times may need to be reduced. Follow the instructions on oven bag packaging.
- Very large cuts of meat will need to be turned halfway through roasting.
- The best way to tell if a roast is done is to use a meat thermometer. Insert the thermometer into the thickest part of the joint. Be careful not to touch any bone as this will give you an inaccurate reading. The reading should be 60°C for rare, 70°C for medium and 75°C for well-done.
- Rest the roast, covered in foil, for 10 to 15 minutes before carving, so that the juices "settle".
- Carve meat across the grain to ensure tenderness. While carving, hold meat with tongs rather than a fork to prevent juice loss. The best type of knife to use for carving is one with a straight edge, rather than a serrated edge.

tips and tricks will guarantee lip-smacking results.

- Before roasting a chicken, wash it well in cold water, especially inside the cavity. Pat dry inside and out with paper towelling.
- Do not freeze an uncooked, seasoned chicken. Chicken and seasoning can be frozen separately, then thawed before filling chicken with seasoning.
- To test if roast chicken is cooked, prick the thigh flesh where it meets the body with a metal skewer; if the juice that runs out is clear, it's cooked.
- Fill chicken cavity loosely with seasoning just before roasting; it will swell during cooking. Secure chicken cavity closed with toothpicks or small skewers. Any leftover seasoning can be moistened with a little stock and cooked in lightly oiled mini muffin pans, or formed into a roll and wrapped in lightly oiled aluminium foil. Bake the extra stuffing with the roast for the last 20 minutes of cooking time.
- Tuck wing tips under the body of chicken; tie legs together with string to help chicken keep its shape during roasting.
- Baste a roast chicken or turkey only occasionally – frequent basting will result in a pale-coloured bird.
- If using a frozen turkey, allow up to three days to thaw in refrigerator.
- To thaw turkey, cut a small corner off the bag in which it is frozen, place turkey in dish. Stand turkey on slight angle so liquid will drain out of bag as turkey defrosts. Discard the liquid from the dish as it accumulates.
- If keeping a cooked chicken overnight, remove any seasoning from the cavity and refrigerate separately.

raan

2 teaspoons coriander seeds
1 teaspoon cumin seeds
8 cardamom pods, bruised
2 cinnamon sticks, crushed
2 star anise
½ teaspoon cracked black pepper
6 cloves
4 cloves garlic, crushed
1 tablespoon grated fresh ginger
2 tablespoons lemon juice
¼ cup (70g) tomato paste
2kg leg of lamb
½ cup (125ml) boiling water
¼ teaspoon saffron threads or powder

Combine seeds, cardamom, cinnamon, star anise, pepper and cloves in dry hot pan; cook, stirring, until fragrant. Grind or process the cooled spices until crushed.
Combine spice mixture with garlic, ginger, juice and paste in small bowl.
Trim fat from lamb then pierce lamb all over with deep cuts. Rub spice mixture over lamb, pressing firmly into cuts. Place lamb in large shallow dish; cover, refrigerate 3 hours or overnight.
Preheat oven to moderate. Pour combined water and saffron into large baking dish; place lamb on oven rack in dish. Cover with foil; bake in moderate oven 1 hour. Remove and discard foil; bake about 30 minutes or until lamb is well browned and cooked as desired. Stand, covered, 10 minutes before carving.
Serve with salad and yogurt, if desired.

serves 6
per serving 15.2g fat; 1536kJ

traditional roast leg of lamb with garlic and rosemary

2kg leg of lamb
2 sprigs fresh rosemary,
  chopped coarsely
8 cloves garlic,
  sliced thinly
20g butter, softened
1 teaspoon cracked
  black pepper

Preheat oven to moderately hot. Pierce lamb all over with sharp knife; place in large baking dish. **Press** rosemary and garlic firmly into cuts; rub combined butter and pepper over lamb. Bake lamb, uncovered, in moderately hot oven 15 minutes. **Reduce** heat to moderate; bake, uncovered, about 1¼ hours or until cooked as desired. Stand, covered, 10 minutes before carving.

serves 6
per serving 17.7g fat; 1585kJ

herb-crusted lamb

2 racks of lamb
  with 6 cutlets
  in each (900g)
1 cup (70g) fresh
  white breadcrumbs
1 tablespoon finely
  chopped macadamias
1 tablespoon
  coarsely chopped
  fresh rosemary
1 tablespoon coarsely
  chopped fresh thyme
1 tablespoon coarsely
  chopped fresh basil
3 cloves garlic, crushed
1 egg white,
  beaten lightly

Preheat oven to moderately hot. Remove visible fat from lamb racks.

Combine breadcrumbs, nuts, herbs, garlic and egg white in medium bowl.

Place racks of lamb in baking dish; press breadcrumb mixture onto lamb. Bake in moderately hot oven about 25 minutes or until lamb is cooked as desired. Stand, covered, 10 minutes before carving.

serves 4
per serving 13.4g fat; 1206kJ

middle-eastern lamb with olive couscous seasoning

Ask your butcher to butterfly the leg of lamb for you.

2kg leg of lamb, butterflied
1 tablespoon olive oil
⅓ cup (80ml) orange juice
½ teaspoon ground cinnamon
¼ cup (90g) honey
2 cloves garlic, crushed
1½ tablespoons cornflour
2 cups (500ml) beef stock

olive couscous seasoning
½ cup (100g) couscous
½ cup (125ml) boiling water
20g butter
1 small white onion (80g),
    chopped finely
1 teaspoon ground cumin
2 tablespoons flaked
    almonds, toasted
1 small apple (130g), peeled,
    cored, chopped coarsely
1 tablespoon brown sugar
¼ cup (40g) coarsely
    chopped seeded
    black olives

Preheat oven to moderate.

Place lamb on board, pound with meat mallet until lamb is an even thickness. Place olive couscous seasoning in centre of lamb; roll up from short side to enclose seasoning.

Secure lamb with skewers, tie with kitchen string at 2cm intervals. Place lamb on wire rack in baking dish, brush with oil. Bake, uncovered, in moderate oven 1 hour.

Combine juice, cinnamon, honey and garlic in small bowl; brush a little juice mixture over lamb. Return lamb to moderate oven for 30 minutes or until tender; baste with remaining juice mixture several times during cooking. Remove lamb from dish; stand, covered, 10 minutes before carving.

Meanwhile, blend cornflour with a little of the stock in small bowl; stir into juices in baking dish with remaining stock. Stir over heat until mixture boils and thickens; strain. Serve with lamb.

Olive couscous seasoning Combine couscous and the water in heatproof bowl; stand, covered, 5 minutes or until all the liquid has been absorbed. Meanwhile, heat butter in small frying pan, add onion; cook, stirring, until soft. Add cumin, nuts, apple, sugar and olives; cook, stirring, about 3 minutes or until apple is softened slightly. Stir in couscous; cool.

serves 6
per serving 22.3g fat; 2399kJ

perfect roast chicken

We've given a traditional roast chicken recipe a Thai twist by using fresh coriander, kaffir lime leaves and lemon grass to flavour it instead of more commonly used seasonings.

1.5kg whole chicken
100g fresh coriander,
     roots intact
4 kaffir lime leaves, torn
2 sticks lemon grass,
     chopped coarsely
2 kaffir limes, quartered
cooking-oil spray
1 teaspoon salt

Preheat oven to moderately hot. Wash cavity of chicken under cold water; pat dry, inside and out, with absorbent paper.
Chop coriander roots, stems and leaves; place all of the coriander, lime leaves, lemon grass and four of the lime quarters inside the chicken cavity. Tuck wings under chicken; trim skin around chicken neck, secure to underside of chicken with toothpicks. Tie legs together using kitchen string.
Place chicken, breast-side up, on rack inside large baking dish.
Spray chicken all over with cooking-oil spray; sprinkle with salt.
Place enough water in baking dish to come to a 1cm depth.
Bake chicken, uncovered, in moderately hot oven for 1½ hours; cover loosely with foil after 1 hour if chicken starts to overbrown.
Discard cavity filling; serve chicken with remaining lime quarters.

serves 4
per serving 30.9g fat; 1778kJ

pesto chicken with roasted ratatouille

1.5kg chicken
3 medium brown onions
   (450g), quartered
4 small green
   zucchini (360g)
4 small yellow
   zucchini (360g)
1 tablespoon olive oil
6 baby eggplant
   (360g), halved
4 large egg tomatoes
   (360g), halved
4 cloves garlic, bruised

pesto
1½ cups firmly packed
   fresh basil leaves
2 tablespoons
   pine nuts, toasted
2 tablespoons grated
   parmesan cheese
2 tablespoons olive oil

Preheat oven to moderate. Loosen skin of chicken by sliding hand
between skin and flesh. Rub pesto under skin and over chicken;
tuck wings under chicken, tie legs together with kitchen string.
Place chicken and onion in large oiled baking dish; bake, uncovered,
in moderate oven 30 minutes.
Halve zucchini lengthways, then cut in half crossways. Add combined
oil, zucchini, eggplant, tomato and garlic to dish; bake, uncovered,
about 1 hour or until chicken is cooked through and vegetables are tender.
Pesto Blend or process basil, nuts and cheese until finely chopped.
Add oil in a thin stream while motor is operating; blend or process until
well combined. Cover surface tightly with plastic wrap until required.

serves 4
per serving 51.1g fat; 2920kJ

roast beef with yorkshire puddings

If beef does not release enough excess oil during cooking, you may have to use melted butter in the patty-pan holes when making yorkshire puddings.

2kg corner piece beef
    topside roast
2 cups (500ml)
    dry red wine
2 bay leaves
6 black peppercorns
¼ cup (70g)
    seeded mustard
4 cloves garlic, sliced
4 sprigs fresh thyme
1 medium brown
    onion (150g),
    chopped coarsely
2 medium carrots
    (240g), chopped
    coarsely
1 large leek (500g),
    chopped coarsely
2 trimmed sticks
    celery (150g),
    chopped coarsely
1 tablespoon olive oil
2 tablespoons plain flour
1½ cups (375ml)
    beef stock

yorkshire puddings
1 cup (150g) plain flour
½ teaspoon salt
2 eggs, beaten lightly
½ cup (125ml) milk
½ cup (125ml) water

Combine beef, wine, bay leaves, peppercorns, mustard, garlic, thyme and onion in large bowl, cover; refrigerate 3 hours or overnight.
Preheat oven to moderate. Drain beef; reserve 1 cup (250ml) of the marinade.
Combine carrot, leek and celery in large baking dish, place beef on top of vegetables; brush beef with oil. Bake, uncovered, in moderate oven about 1½ hours or until beef is browned and cooked as desired.
Remove beef from dish, wrap in foil; stand 20 minutes before serving.
Meanwhile, remove and discard vegetables with slotted spoon. Pour pan juices into jug, stand 5 minutes then pour off excess oil; reserve 1½ tablespoons of the oil for yorkshire puddings and 2 tablespoons of pan juices for gravy.
Heat reserved pan juices for gravy in same baking dish, add flour; cook, stirring, until bubbling. Gradually add reserved marinade and stock; cook, stirring, until mixture boils and thickens.
Strain gravy into heatproof jug. Serve beef with gravy and yorkshire puddings.
Yorkshire puddings Sift flour and salt into medium bowl, make well in centre; add combined egg, milk and water all at once. Using wooden spoon, gradually stir in flour from side of bowl until batter is smooth. Cover; allow to stand 30 minutes. Divide the reserved oil among 12-hole (2 tablespoon/40ml) patty pan; heat in hot oven 2 minutes. Divide batter among pan holes; bake about 15 minutes or until puddings are golden.

serves 8
per serving 15.6g fat; 2131kJ

honey chicken with roasted capsicum

1.5kg whole chicken
2 medium red
    capsicum (400g)
2 medium yellow
    capsicum (400g)

honey glaze
½ cup (175g) honey
¼ cup (60ml) soy sauce
1 tablespoon grated
    fresh ginger
½ teaspoon sesame oil
½ teaspoon
    five-spice powder

Preheat oven to moderate. Place chicken in baking dish, brush with
honey glaze; cover with greased foil. Bake in moderate oven 45 minutes.
Cut capsicum into 3cm pieces, add to dish; bake, covered, 30 minutes.
Remove foil; bake, uncovered, for 15 minutes or until chicken is cooked
through, brushing occasionally with pan juices during cooking.
Serve chicken with capsicum and pan juices.
Honey glaze Combine ingredients in small bowl.

serves 4
per serving 31g fat; 2529kJ

portuguese chicken

1.5kg whole chicken
4 fresh red thai
  chillies, seeded,
  chopped finely
1 tablespoon
  sweet paprika
2 teaspoons
  dried oregano
2 teaspoons salt
1 tablespoon
  brown sugar
½ cup (125ml)
  lemon juice
2 tablespoons olive oil

Using kitchen scissors, cut along both sides of backbone of chicken; discard backbone. Place chicken, skin-side up, on board; using heel of hand, press on breastbone to flatten chicken. Wash chicken under cold water; pat dry with absorbent paper.

Combine chilli, paprika, oregano, salt, sugar, juice and oil in small jug; pour over chicken in large shallow dish. Cover; refrigerate 3 hours or overnight.

Preheat oven to hot. Drain chicken; reserve marinade. Place chicken on oiled wire rack over baking dish; pour over reserved marinade.

Bake, uncovered, in hot oven, brushing occasionally with pan juices, about 1¼ hours or until chicken is browned and cooked through.

serves 4
per serving 39.6g fat; 2203kJ

gremolata-crumbed roast leg of lamb

1.7kg leg of lamb
¼ cup (60ml) lemon juice
4 cloves garlic, crushed
5 large potatoes (1.5kg)
1 medium brown onion (150g), chopped finely
2 trimmed sticks celery (150g), chopped finely
2 tablespoons plain flour
½ cup (125ml) dry red wine
2 cups (500ml) beef stock
2 sprigs fresh rosemary
1 tablespoon finely chopped fresh flat-leaf parsley

gremolata
½ cup finely chopped fresh flat-leaf parsley
1 tablespoon grated lemon rind
2 cloves garlic, crushed
½ cup (35g) stale breadcrumbs
1 tablespoon olive oil

Combine lamb with juice and half of the garlic in large bowl. Cover; refrigerate 3 hours or overnight, turning lamb occasionally in marinade.
Preheat oven to moderate. Cut each potato into eight wedges. Place undrained lamb and potato in large flameproof baking dish; bake, uncovered, in moderate oven 1 hour.
Press gremolata mixture onto lamb; bake, uncovered, in moderate oven about 30 minutes or until lamb is cooked as desired. Remove lamb and potato from baking dish; stand, covered, in warm place, 10 minutes before serving.
Cook onion, celery and remaining garlic in baking dish, stirring, until vegetables are soft. Stir in flour; cook, stirring, 1 minute or until bubbling. Gradually stir in wine and stock, add rosemary; cook, stirring, until gravy thickens. Strain gravy into medium jug. Serve lamb and potato with gravy; sprinkle with parsley.
Gremolata Combine ingredients in small bowl.

serves 6
per serving 16.4g fat; 2247kJ

chicken risoni

1.5kg whole chicken
2 cloves garlic, crushed
2 tablespoons olive oil
1 medium brown
    onion (150g),
    chopped coarsely
500g celeriac,
    grated coarsely
2 cups (500ml)
    chicken stock
2 x 400g cans tomatoes
1 cup (220g) risoni
2 bay leaves
2 teaspoons grated
    lemon rind
1 tablespoon finely
    chopped fresh
    flat-leaf parsley
1 tablespoon
    finely chopped
    fresh oregano
2/3 cup (80g) seeded
    black olives

Preheat oven to moderate. Wash chicken under cold water; pat dry with absorbent paper. Tuck wings under chicken; tie legs together with kitchen string.
Place chicken, breast-side up, in oiled baking dish. Brush with combined garlic and half of the oil; bake, uncovered, in moderate oven for 1 hour.
Meanwhile, heat remaining oil in large frying pan; cook onion, stirring, until soft. Add celeriac; cook, stirring, about 5 minutes or until celeriac is tender. Stir in stock, undrained crushed tomatoes, pasta, bay leaves and rind. Bring to a boil; simmer, stirring occasionally, about 10 minutes or until mixture thickens slightly.
Pour tomato mixture around chicken in baking dish; bake, uncovered, about 30 minutes or until pasta is tender and chicken cooked through.
Stir parsley, oregano and olives through pasta.

serves 4
per serving 39.6g fat; 3218kJ

spatchcocks with prosciutto and herb butter

2 x 500g spatchcocks
6 sprigs fresh thyme
2 large slices
   prosciutto (45g)
1 tablespoon olive oil
1 tablespoon lemon juice

herb butter
30g butter, softened
1 clove garlic, crushed
1 tablespoon finely
   chopped fresh
   flat-leaf parsley
1 tablespoon finely
   chopped fresh basil

Preheat oven to hot. Wash spatchcocks under cold water; pat dry with absorbent paper.
Loosen skin of spatchcock by carefully sliding fingers between skin and flesh; spoon quarter of the herb butter under skin of each spatchcock and press over breast with fingers. Place a sprig of thyme inside each cavity and tie legs together with kitchen string. Wrap prosciutto around the centre of spatchcocks, securing with a toothpick.
Place spatchcocks in baking dish; drizzle with combined oil and juice. Bake in hot oven 30 minutes. Brush spatchcocks with pan juices; top with remaining thyme sprigs. Bake 20 minutes or until spatchcocks are cooked through. Serve spatchcocks topped with remaining herb butter.
Herb butter Combine ingredients in a small bowl.

serves 2
per serving 63g fat; 3270kJ

spicy roast spatchcocks

4 x 500g spatchcocks
2 teaspoons sweet paprika
2 cloves garlic, crushed
1 teaspoon cumin seeds
2 teaspoons yellow mustard seeds
2 tablespoons finely chopped
   fresh coriander
2 green onions, chopped finely
$\frac{1}{3}$ cup (110g) mango chutney
2 tablespoons olive oil

vinaigrette
$\frac{1}{3}$ cup (80ml) olive oil
2 tablespoons lemon juice
$\frac{1}{2}$ teaspoon sugar

Using kitchen scissors, cut along each side of spatchcock backbone; discard backbones. Cut spatchcocks in half along breastbones.
Combine spatchcocks in bowl with paprika, garlic, seeds, coriander, onion, chutney and oil. Cover, refrigerate 3 hours or overnight.
Preheat oven to hot. Drain spatchcocks; reserve marinade.
Place spatchcocks, skin-side up, on rack in baking dish. Bake, uncovered, in hot oven about 30 minutes or until spatchcocks are cooked through, brushing with reserved marinade several times during cooking. Serve spatchcocks drizzled with vinaigrette.
Vinaigrette Combine ingredients in screw-topped jar.

serves 4
per serving 66g fat; 4287kJ

slow-roasted greek lamb with lemon and potatoes

This style of slow-roasting produces well-cooked but very moist, tender meat which literally falls off the bone. This may make it difficult to carve, in which case simply cut into chunks to serve.

2kg leg of lamb
3 cloves garlic, quartered
6 sprigs fresh oregano, halved
salt, pepper
1 large lemon (180g)
5 medium potatoes (1kg), quartered lengthways

Preheat oven to slow. Make 12 small cuts in the lamb with a sharp knife. Press garlic and oregano into cuts. Rub lamb with salt and pepper.
Remove rind from lemon and cut rind into long thin strips (or remove rind with a zester). Squeeze juice from lemon – you will need $^1/_3$ cup (80ml) of juice.
Place lamb upside down in large baking dish, pour lemon juice over lamb. Cover dish tightly with foil; bake in slow oven for 2 hours. Turn lamb over, brush all over with pan juices; sprinkle with lemon rind. Cover dish; bake 30 minutes.
Add potato to dish; bake, covered, for 1¾ hours. Remove foil; bake, uncovered, about 15 minutes or until browned. Stand lamb and potato, covered, in warm place, 10 minutes before serving.

serves 8
per serving 11.3g fat; 1409kJ

garlic roasted duck

A duck wing portion consists of the wing and part of the breast.

2 tablespoons fish sauce
4 cloves garlic, crushed
1 cup (250ml) red
  wine vinegar
1 large brown
  onion (200g),
  coarsely chopped
2 teaspoons juniper
  berries, bruised
2 teaspoons fennel seeds
4 duck wing
  portions (1.5kg)
2 tablespoons yogurt

Combine fish sauce, garlic, vinegar, onion, berries and seeds in medium bowl. Place duck in single layer in shallow dish; pour over vinegar mixture. Cover dish; refrigerate 3 hours or overnight.

Preheat oven to moderate. Remove duck from marinade; reserve marinade.

Place duck, skin-side up, on wire rack over baking dish; bake, uncovered, in moderate oven about 45 minutes or until tender.

Place reserved marinade in small saucepan; simmer, uncovered, about 5 minutes or until slightly thickened, strain. Stir yogurt into sauce; serve with duck.

serves 4
per serving 75.4g fat; 3397kJ

slow-roasted lamb shanks with caramelised red onion

1 tablespoon olive oil
8 french-trimmed lamb shanks (1.2kg)
1 tablespoon sugar
1½ cups (375ml) dry red wine
2 cups (500ml) beef stock
3 cloves garlic, crushed
20g butter
1 small brown onion (80g), chopped finely
1 trimmed celery stick (75g), chopped finely
1 tablespoon plain flour
1 tablespoon tomato paste
4 sprigs fresh rosemary, chopped coarsely

caramelised onion
40g butter
2 medium red onions (340g), sliced thinly
¼ cup (50g) brown sugar
¼ cup (60ml) balsamic vinegar

Preheat oven to slow. Heat oil in large flameproof baking dish; cook lamb until browned all over. Stir in sugar, wine, stock and garlic; bring to a boil. Transfer lamb to slow oven; bake, covered, 4 hours, turning twice during cooking. Remove lamb from dish; cover to keep warm. Pour liquid from dish into large heatproof jug.

Return dish to heat, melt butter; cook onion and celery, stirring, until celery is just tender. Stir in flour; cook, stirring, 2 minutes. Add reserved liquid, tomato paste and rosemary; bring to a boil. Simmer, uncovered, stirring until mixture boils and thickens; strain wine sauce into large heatproof jug. Serve lamb with wine sauce and caramelised onion.

Caramelised onion Melt butter in medium saucepan; cook onion, stirring, about 15 minutes or until browned and soft. Stir in sugar and vinegar; cook, stirring, about 15 minutes or until onion is caramelised.

serves 4
per serving 32g fat; 2510kJ

chinese roast pork neck

2kg piece pork neck
¼ cup (60ml) soy sauce
2 tablespoons dry sherry
1 tablespoon
   brown sugar
1 tablespoon honey
1 teaspoon red
   food colouring
1 clove garlic, crushed
½ teaspoon five-spice
   powder

Halve pork lengthways. Combine pork in large bowl with remaining ingredients, cover; refrigerate 3 hours or overnight.
Preheat oven to hot. Drain pork; reserve marinade.
Place pork on wire rack in baking dish; bake, uncovered, in hot oven 30 minutes. Reduce heat to moderate; bake, uncovered, about 1 hour or until pork is browned and cooked through, brushing occasionally with reserved marinade. Stand pork, covered, 10 minutes before slicing.

serves 6
per serving 12.7g fat; 1815kJ

roast beef and vegetables in an oven bag

4 cloves garlic, peeled
1.8kg corner piece
  beef topside roast
12 small sprigs
  fresh thyme
6 medium carrots
  (720g), halved
12 baby onions
  (300g), peeled
1 tablespoon
  seeded mustard
¼ cup (90g) honey
1 tablespoon olive oil

Preheat oven to moderate. Cut each garlic clove into three slices. Make 12 small slits on fat side of beef; insert garlic and thyme into slits. Cut a narrow strip from the top of 35cm x 48cm oven bag to use as a tie. Place beef, carrot and onion in bag. Add combined remaining ingredients to bag; close end with tie.

Gently turn bag to coat beef and vegetables with mustard mixture. Place bag in large baking dish, pierce three holes near tie end; bake in moderate oven about 1½ hours or until beef is cooked as desired. Carefully remove beef and vegetables from bag; stand, covered, in warm place, 10 minutes before serving.

Pour juices from oven bag into baking dish; simmer, uncovered, until reduced to ½ cup (125ml). Serve beef and vegetables drizzled with mustard mixture.

serves 6
per serving 15.9g fat; 2051kJ

rack of pork with apple sauce

Kipfler are small finger-shaped potatoes. You can use halved desiree or pontiac potatoes if you prefer.

coarse salt
1.3kg pork rack (6 cutlets)
1.25kg kipfler potatoes
750g pumpkin, chopped coarsely
1 tablespoon olive oil

apple sauce
3 large green apples (600g)
¼ cup (60ml) water
4 fresh sage leaves
1 teaspoon sugar

Preheat oven to very hot. Rub salt evenly into rind of pork. Cover bones with foil to prevent burning. Place pork, rind-side up, in large baking dish; bake, uncovered, in very hot oven about 35 minutes or until rind is blistered and browned.

Place potatoes and pumpkin in separate baking dish, drizzle with oil. Reduce oven temperature to moderate; bake pork and vegetables, uncovered, about 40 minutes or until pork is cooked through. Remove pork from dish; cover with foil to keep warm.

Increase oven temperature to very hot; bake vegetables for 15 minutes or until browned and tender. Serve pork with vegetables and apple sauce.

Apple sauce Peel and core apples; cut into thick slices. Combine apple, the water and sage in medium saucepan; simmer, uncovered, about 10 minutes or until apple is soft. Remove from heat, stir in sugar.

serves 6
per serving 11.4g fat; 1765kJ

fig and orange glazed ham

8kg cooked leg ham
60 whole cloves,
   approximately

fig and orange glaze
1 cup (320g) fig jam
2 tablespoons
   dijon mustard
⅓ cup (80ml)
   orange juice
2 tablespoons brandy

Cut a circle in rind of ham about 10cm from shank end. To remove rind, run your thumb around edges of rind just under skin. Start pulling rind from widest edge of ham; continue to pull rind carefully away from fat up to cut at shank end. Use reserved rind to cover the cut surface of ham to keep it moist during storage.

Preheat oven to moderate. Using a sharp knife, score across fat at about 3cm intervals, cutting just through surface of fat. Do not cut deeply into fat, or it will spread apart during cooking. Score in opposite direction to make a diamond pattern; stud with cloves.

Place ham on wire rack in large baking dish; cover shank with foil. Brush ham with half of the fig and orange glaze; bake, uncovered, in moderate oven about 1¼ hours or until browned, brushing often with remaining glaze during cooking.

Fig and orange glaze Combine jam, mustard, juice and brandy in small saucepan; stir over low heat, without boiling, until jam melts.

serves 16
per serving 28.2g fat; 2416kJ

garlic and rosemary roasted vegetables

3 golden nugget
  pumpkins (1.2kg)
1.5kg baby
  new potatoes
800g spring
  onions, trimmed
8 cloves garlic, unpeeled
2 tablespoons olive oil
¼ cup fresh rosemary

Preheat oven to moderate. Cut pumpkins into quarters; remove and discard seeds. Cut each quarter in half.

Combine pumpkin, potatoes, onion, garlic, oil and half of the rosemary in large baking dish; bake in moderate oven about 1½ hours or until vegetables are browned and tender. Serve roasted vegetables sprinkled with remaining rosemary.

serves 8
per serving 5.5g fat; 1000kJ

straight to the sauce

A good sauce can turn a plain roast into something sublime. These recipes will ensure your roasts are unforgettable.

gravy

1 small brown onion (80g), chopped finely
2 tablespoons plain flour
½ cup (125ml) dry red wine
1½ cups (375ml) chicken or beef stock

Remove roast from baking dish, cover to keep warm. Reserve 2 tablespoons of juices in baking dish; discard remaining juice.
Add onion to dish; cook, stirring, until soft. Stir in flour; cook, stirring, about 5 minutes or until browned. Pour in wine and stock; cook over high heat, stirring, until gravy boils and thickens. Strain gravy before serving.

makes 2 cups (500ml)
per tablespoon 0.1g fat; 40kJ

tip To adapt this gravy into peppercorn or mushroom gravy, place strained gravy in small saucepan; add 1 tablespoon drained canned green peppercorns or 100g finely sliced cooked button mushrooms. Cook, stirring, 2 minutes.

devilled sauce

1 tablespoon olive oil
1 medium brown onion (150g), chopped finely
2 cloves garlic, crushed
1 teaspoon hot paprika
¼ cup (50g) firmly packed brown sugar
⅓ cup (80ml) cider vinegar
1 teaspoon Tabasco sauce
1 tablespoon worcestershire sauce
2 cups (500ml) beef stock
1 tablespoon cornflour
1 tablespoon water

Heat oil in medium frying pan, add onion and garlic; cook, stirring, until onion is soft. Stir in paprika, sugar and vinegar; cook, stirring, without boiling, until sugar dissolves.
Add sauces and stock; simmer, uncovered, about 15 minutes or until reduced to 2 cups. Stir in blended cornflour and water; stir until sauce boils and thickens.

makes 2 cups (500ml)
per tablespoon 0.8g fat; 91kJ

traditional mint sauce

1 cup (250ml) cider vinegar
¼ cup (60ml) boiling water
¼ cup finely chopped fresh
  mint leaves
1 tablespoon brown sugar
1 teaspoon salt
¼ teaspoon ground black pepper

Combine ingredients in small bowl;
stand 30 minutes before serving.

makes 1¼ cups (310ml)
per tablespoon 0g fat; 25kJ

apple sauce

2 small apples (260g)
2 tablespoons sugar
½ cup (125ml) water
pinch ground cinnamon

Peel apples; cut into quarters.
Remove core; slice apple.
Combine apple, sugar, the water and
cinnamon in small saucepan, cover;
bring to a boil. Reduce heat; simmer,
covered, about 5 minutes or until apple
is pulpy. Whisk until sauce is smooth.

makes 1 cup (250ml)
per tablespoon 0g fat; 74kJ

tunnel-boned lamb with coriander hazelnut pesto

Ask the butcher to bone the lamb shoulder for you.

⅓ cup (50g) unroasted hazelnuts
½ cup firmly packed fresh coriander leaves
⅓ cup firmly packed fresh basil leaves
1 tablespoon grated fresh ginger
5 cloves garlic, crushed
2 tablespoons lime juice
2 teaspoons fish sauce
1 teaspoon brown sugar
2 tablespoons olive oil
1.7kg lamb shoulder, boned

Preheat oven to moderately hot. Spread nuts
in a single layer on oven tray; toast, uncovered,
in moderately hot oven about 5 minutes or until
skins begin to flake. Rub hazelnuts in soft cloth
to remove skins; cool.
Reduce oven temperature to moderate. Blend or
process nuts, herbs, ginger, garlic, juice, sauce
and sugar until pureed. With motor operating,
pour in oil; process until pesto thickens.
Spread lamb with half of the pesto. Roll from
short side to enclose pesto; secure lamb with
skewers, tie with kitchen string at 2cm intervals.
Place lamb on wire rack in large baking dish.
Spread remaining pesto onto outside of lamb.
Bake, uncovered, in moderate oven about
1¾ hours or until cooked as desired. Stand lamb,
covered, 10 minutes before carving.

serves 6
per serving 23.3g fat; 1635kJ

slow-roasted salmon

750g piece salmon fillet,
   boned, with skin on
1 tablespoon finely
   shredded kaffir
   lime leaves
¼ cup (55g)
   caster sugar
2 tablespoons lime juice
2 tablespoons water
1 fresh red thai
   chilli, seeded,
   chopped finely
1 tablespoon
   coarsely chopped
   fresh coriander

Preheat oven to very slow. Cook fish on heated
oiled grill plate until browned both sides. Place
fish in large oiled baking dish, sprinkle with lime
leaves; bake, covered tightly, in very slow oven
about 30 minutes or until cooked as desired.
Meanwhile, combine sugar, juice and the water in
small saucepan; stir over heat, without boiling, until
sugar dissolves. Simmer, uncovered, without stirring,
2 minutes; cool slightly, stir in chilli and coriander.
Serve fish drizzled with chilli sauce.

serves 4
per serving 13.3g fat; 1345kJ

traditional roast potatoes

5 medium potatoes (1kg)
2 tablespoons olive oil
40g butter, melted
1 teaspoon salt

Preheat oven to hot. Cut potatoes into uniformly-sized pieces.
Cook potato in large saucepan of boiling water 5 minutes. Drain; cool on absorbent paper.
Combine potato, oil and butter in large baking dish. Sprinkle with salt; bake in hot oven about 1 hour or until tender.

serves 4
per serving 17.5g fat; 1222kJ

slow-roasted turkey with port gravy

4kg turkey
¼ cup (60ml) chicken stock
½ cup (125ml) port
2 tablespoons brown sugar
2 tablespoons vegetable oil
2 tablespoons plain flour

seasoning
2 tablespoons vegetable oil
2 medium brown onions (300g), sliced
500g sausage mince
4 cups (280g) stale breadcrumbs
2 tablespoons chopped fresh sage
½ cup (60g) chopped walnuts

Preheat oven to slow. Discard neck and giblets from turkey. Rinse turkey under cold water; pat dry inside and out, tuck wings under body. Spoon seasoning loosely into cavity. Tie legs together with kitchen string.
Place turkey into oiled flameproof baking dish; pour stock and half of the port into dish. Cover baking dish tightly with greased foil (if thin, use two layers); bake in slow oven for 5½ hours. Remove foil, brush turkey with combined remaining port and sugar. Increase temperature to moderate; bake, uncovered, 30 minutes or until browned.
Remove turkey from dish; cover with foil to keep warm. Strain juices from dish into jug; remove fat from juices. You will need 3 cups (750ml) pan juices. Heat oil in same baking dish, stir in flour; stir over heat until well browned. Remove from heat, gradually stir in reserved pan juices; stir over heat until gravy boils and thickens, strain. Serve turkey with gravy.
Seasoning Heat oil in large frying pan, add onion; cook, stirring, until browned, cool. Transfer onion to medium bowl; stir in remaining ingredients.

serves 8
per serving 62.1g fat; 4105kJ

roasted vegetables

6 medium tomatoes (1kg)
3 medium
   potatoes (600g)
3 medium red
   onions (510g)
4 medium
   zucchini (480g)
2 trimmed celery
   sticks (150g)
⅓ cup finely chopped
   fresh flat-leaf parsley
2 tablespoons finely
   chopped fresh dill
2 cloves garlic, crushed
2 tablespoons olive oil

Preheat oven to hot. Cut tomatoes into thin slices. Cut potatoes and onions into wedges. Cut zucchini in half lengthways, then into 3cm lengths. Cut celery into 3cm lengths.
Lightly oil baking dish, add half of the tomato, top with potato, onion, zucchini and celery. Place remaining tomato over vegetables. Sprinkle with herbs and garlic; drizzle with oil.
Bake, uncovered, in hot oven 30 minutes or until vegetables are tender.

serves 6
per serving 6.7g fat; 771kJ

chipped potatoes with malt vinegar

5 medium potatoes (1kg)
1 tablespoon olive oil
2 egg whites,
   beaten lightly
sea salt and freshly
   ground black pepper
⅓ cup (80ml) brown
   malt vinegar

Preheat oven to hot. Slice potatoes thinly.
Toss potato in combined oil and egg white. Place in a single layer in an oiled baking dish; sprinkle with salt and pepper. Bake, uncovered, in hot oven about 30 minutes or until potato is golden and crisp.
Serve drizzled with malt vinegar.

serves 6
per serving 3.2g fat; 528kJ

spiced beef with chilli jam

1 tablespoon cumin seeds
1 tablespoon coriander seeds
1 teaspoon cardamom seeds
750g beef eye fillet

chilli jam
2 tablespoons olive oil
2 medium red capsicums (400g), chopped
2 small tomatoes (260g), chopped
3 small brown onions (300g), chopped
4 red thai chillies, seeded, chopped
3 cloves garlic, crushed
½ cup (125ml) white wine vinegar
½ cup (110g) caster sugar
¼ cup (50g) brown sugar
1 tablespoon balsamic vinegar

Place seeds in a dry frying pan; stir over low heat until fragrant. Grind or blend spices until crushed.
Roll beef in spices, cover; refrigerate beef 3 hours or overnight.
Preheat oven to moderate. Place beef in oiled baking dish; bake, uncovered, in moderate oven about 45 minutes or until cooked as desired. Stand, covered, 10 minutes before carving. Serve beef with chilli jam.
Chilli jam Heat oil in large saucepan, add capsicum, tomato, onion, chilli and garlic; cook, stirring, over low heat, about 20 minutes or until capsicum is soft. Add white wine vinegar and caster sugar; stir over heat, without boiling, until sugar dissolves. Simmer, uncovered, about 15 minutes or until mixture is thick. Stir in brown sugar and balsamic vinegar; blend or process mixture until roughly chopped. Spoon into hot sterilised jar, seal while hot; cool, refrigerate.

serves 4
per serving 19.1g fat; 2293kJ

roasted root vegetables

1 tablespoon olive oil
10 baby carrots (200g),
    peeled, halved
    lengthways
2 small parsnips (120g),
    peeled, quartered
    lengthways
8 baby potatoes
    (320g), halved
3 baby onions
    (75g), halved
1 clove garlic, crushed
1 tablespoon fresh
    rosemary
1 tablespoon honey
2 teaspoons
    seeded mustard
1 tablespoon lemon juice

Preheat oven to hot. Heat oil in flameproof
baking dish on stove-top. Place carrot, parsnip,
potato and onion in baking dish; cook over heat
until lightly browned, turning occasionally.
Remove from heat; stir in garlic, rosemary,
honey and mustard.
Bake in hot oven about 20 minutes or until
vegetables are tender. Serve drizzled with
lemon juice.

serves 2
per serving 9.7g fat; 1274kJ

honey-mustard glazed kumara

2 large kumara (1kg)
6 baby onions
  (150g), halved
½ cup (125ml) honey
2 tablespoons
  balsamic vinegar
2 tablespoons
  seeded mustard
1 tablespoon water
1 tablespoon peanut oil
1 tablespoon grated
  fresh ginger
50g baby rocket leaves

Preheat oven to moderately hot. Slice kumara
into 1cm-thick rounds. Place kumara and onion in
large bowl; toss with combined honey, vinegar,
mustard, water, oil and ginger. Drain vegetables;
reserve honey mixture.

Place vegetables on wire rack over foil-covered
oven tray. Bake in moderately hot oven about
35 minutes, brushing frequently during cooking
with honey mixture, or until vegetables are
browned lightly. Serve vegetables with rocket.

serves 4
per serving 5.2g fat; 1542kJ

slow-roasted veal breast with soft polenta

2 tablespoons olive oil
20g butter
2kg veal breast
2 medium brown onions (300g), chopped coarsely
2 cloves garlic, quartered
2 medium carrots (240g), chopped
4 trimmed sticks celery (300g), chopped coarsely
6 sprigs fresh rosemary
1 cup (250ml) dry white wine
1 cup (250ml) beef stock

soft polenta
1.5 litres (6 cups) water
2 teaspoons salt
2 cups (340g) polenta
½ cup (125ml) milk
½ cup (40g) grated parmesan cheese

Heat oil and butter in large flameproof baking dish; cook veal until browned all over, remove from dish. Add onion and garlic to same dish; cook, stirring, until soft.

Stir in carrot, celery and rosemary; cook, stirring, until softened slightly. Add combined wine and stock to dish; bring to a boil.

Meanwhile, preheat oven to moderately slow. Return veal to dish with vegetables; bake, tightly covered, in moderately slow oven about 3 hours or until tender. Slice veal and serve with soft polenta; top with vegetables and drizzle with pan juices.

Soft polenta Bring the water and salt to a boil in large saucepan. Gradually stir in polenta then simmer, uncovered, about 25 minutes or until thick, stirring constantly. Add milk; cook, stirring, about 5 minutes or until mixture is thick. Stir in cheese.

serves 8
per serving 15.9g fat; 2304kJ

roasted tomatoes with balsamic dressing

12 large egg
   tomatoes (1kg),
   halved lengthways
⅓ cup (80ml) olive oil
1 tablespoon sugar
2 cloves garlic, crushed
1 teaspoon salt
1 teaspoon cracked
   black pepper
1 tablespoon
   balsamic vinegar
1 tablespoon shredded
   fresh basil leaves

Preheat oven to moderate.
Place tomato, cut-side up, on wire rack in
baking dish. Brush with half of the combined
oil, sugar, garlic, salt and pepper.
Bake, uncovered, in moderate oven about
1½ hours or until tomato is softened and
browned lightly.
Drizzle combined remaining oil and vinegar
over tomatoes; scatter with basil.

serves 6
per serving 12.3g fat; 596kJ

roasted garlic celeriac

1 large celeriac (1.5kg)
2 tablespoons olive oil
1 medium bulb
   garlic (70g)
⅓ cup coarsely chopped
   fresh flat-leaf parsley
⅓ cup (95g)
   low-fat yogurt

Preheat oven to
moderate. Peel
celeriac, cut into
3cm chunks; combine
with oil in large bowl.
Place celeriac and
unpeeled garlic bulb
on baking-paper-lined
oven tray; bake in
moderate oven,
turning occasionally,
about 1 hour or until
celeriac is tender
and golden brown.
Cut garlic bulb in half
horizontally, squeeze
garlic pulp from each
clove over celeriac;
toss together with
parsley. Serve celeriac
topped with yogurt.

serves 4
per serving
10.6g fat; 885kJ

honey-glazed pork with sage

*Ask your butcher to remove the rind completely
from the pork loin and score it.*

2.5kg boned loin of pork
2 teaspoons vegetable oil
1 tablespoon salt
2 cloves garlic, crushed
1 tablespoon finely chopped fresh sage
1/3 cup (90g) honey, warmed
1 tablespoon red wine vinegar
2 cups (500ml) chicken stock
2 tablespoons cornflour
2 tablespoons water

Preheat oven to very hot. Lay pork rind, fat-side down,
on wire rack in large flameproof baking dish; rub oil
and salt into it. Bake, uncovered, in very hot oven
about 30 minutes or until the crackling is crisp and
browned; cool. Discard fat from baking dish.
Lay pork, fat-side down, on board; sprinkle with half of
the garlic and half of the sage. Roll pork to enclose sage
and garlic; secure with kitchen string at 2cm intervals.
Place pork on wire rack in large flameproof baking dish.
Reduce oven temperature to moderately hot; bake pork,
uncovered, 30 minutes. Cover pork with foil, reduce
oven temperature to moderate; bake 1 hour.
Combine honey, vinegar and remaining sage and
garlic in small bowl. Remove foil from pork, brush pork
with half of the honey mixture. Bake pork, uncovered,
30 minutes or until browned and cooked through,
brushing occasionally with remaining honey mixture.
Remove pork from dish; cover with foil.
Strain pan juices from baking dish into heatproof jug;
remove fat from pan juices (you will need 2/3 cup of pan
juices). Add stock to baking dish with pan juices. Stir in
combined cornflour and water; stir until sauce boils and
thickens. Serve pork slices with sauce and crackling.

serves 8
per serving 71.1g fat; 3802kJ

roasted capsicum with port and basil dressing

2 medium red capsicums (400g)
2 medium green capsicums (400g)
2 medium yellow capsicums (400g)
10 green onions
8 cloves garlic
4 small white onions (400g), quartered
1 tablespoon olive oil

port and basil dressing
½ cup (125ml) olive oil
¼ cup (60ml) balsamic vinegar
2 cloves garlic
⅓ cup firmly packed fresh basil leaves
1 tablespoon port
1 tablespoon mild chilli sauce

Preheat oven to moderate. Quarter capsicums; remove and discard seeds and membranes.
Combine with remaining ingredients in large baking dish; bake, uncovered, in moderate oven 1 hour.
Serve warm capsicum mixture with port and basil dressing.
Port and basil dressing Blend or process ingredients until pureed.

serves 8
per serving 33.8g fat; 1645kJ

baked fish with ginger and soy

800g whole snapper
1 tablespoon grated
   fresh ginger
1 tablespoon peanut oil
¼ cup (60ml) chinese
   rice wine
¼ cup (60ml) soy sauce
½ teaspoon sugar
3 green onions,
   sliced thinly

Preheat oven to moderately hot. Cut three deep slits in each side of fish; place fish in oiled baking dish.
Rub ginger into fish; drizzle with combined oil, wine, sauce and sugar. Bake, covered, in moderately hot oven about 25 minutes or until fish is cooked through.
Serve fish drizzled with some of the pan juices and topped with onion.

serves 2
per serving
11.6g fat; 1181kJ

roasted beetroot and onion

2 tablespoons olive oil
10 medium unpeeled fresh
    beetroot (1.6kg), halved
20 baby onions (500g), peeled
2 tablespoons red wine vinegar
2 tablespoons olive oil, extra
freshly ground black pepper
2 tablespoons coarsely chopped
    fresh flat-leaf parsley

Preheat oven to very hot.
Brush base of baking dish with
half of the oil, add beetroot; cover
tightly with foil. Bake in very hot
oven 45 minutes.
Combine onions with remaining
oil. Add onions to beetroot in dish;
cover tightly with foil. Bake in
very hot oven 30 minutes or until
vegetables are tender. Remove
foil; cook 10 minutes.
Wearing rubber gloves, remove
skin from hot beetroot. Cut beetroot
in half . Place beetroot and onion
in serving dish; drizzle with
combined vinegar and extra oil,
sprinkle with pepper and parsley.

serves 6
per serving 12.5g fat; 971kJ

whole roast snapper with lemon and currant pilaf

500g baby beetroot, trimmed
1 whole snapper (1.5kg)
2 teaspoons olive oil
50g baby rocket leaves

lemon and currant pilaf
2 cups (500ml) chicken stock
1 tablespoon grated lemon rind
1 cup (200g) long-grain rice
⅔ cup (100g) dried currants

Preheat oven to hot. Place beetroot in oiled baking dish; bake in hot oven about 20 minutes or until tender. Allow beetroot to cool; peel, grate coarsely.
Reduce oven temperature to moderately hot. Cut three shallow slashes across fish on both sides. Fill cavity with lemon and currant pilaf, brush with oil; place fish in large oiled baking dish.
Bake, uncovered, in moderately hot oven about 30 minutes or until fish is cooked. Serve with beetroot and rocket.
Lemon and currant pilaf Combine stock and rind in large saucepan, bring to a boil; add rice, reduce heat to low. Simmer, covered, about 15 minutes or until liquid is absorbed and rice is tender. Stir in currants.

serves 4
per serving 9.4g fat; 2054kJ

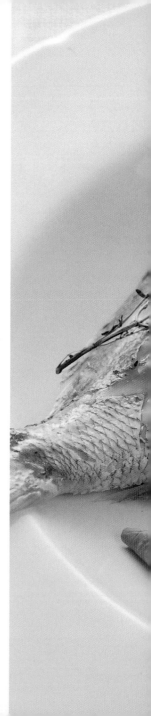

roasted mushrooms

500g button mushrooms
500g swiss brown mushrooms
3 cloves garlic, crushed
2 tablespoons olive oil
2 teaspoons salt
½ teaspoon freshly ground black pepper

Preheat oven to hot. Combine
ingredients in large bowl; place
mixture in single layer in baking dish.
Bake, uncovered, in hot oven about
20 minutes or until mushrooms are
very soft and browned lightly.

serves 6
per serving 6.6g fat; 395kJ

glossary

beetroot also known as red beets; firm, round root vegetable. Smaller beetroots are also available, sold as baby beetroots.

breadcrumbs

fresh: fresh bread made into crumbs by grating, blending or processing.

stale: one- or two-day-old bread made into crumbs by grating, blending or processing.

butter use salted or unsalted (sweet) butter; 125g is equal to one stick of butter.

capsicum also known as bell pepper or, simply, pepper. Seeds and membranes should be discarded before use.

cardamom available in pod, seed or ground form; has a distinctive, aromatic, sweetly rich flavour.

celeriac a thick tuberous root vegetable with brown skin and white flesh, with a celery-like flavour.

chillies available in many different types and sizes. Use rubber gloves when seeding and chopping fresh chillies as they can burn your skin. Removing seeds and membranes lessens the heat level.

chinese rice wine sweet, gold-coloured, low-alcohol wine made from fermented rice; substitute dry sherry if unavailable.

cooking-oil spray we used a cholesterol-free cooking spray made from canola oil.

cornflour also known as cornstarch; used as a thickening agent in cooking.

couscous fine, grain-like cereal product, made from semolina.

cumin also known as zeera.

dried mixed herbs a blend of dried, crushed thyme, rosemary, marjoram, basil, oregano and sage.

eggplant also known as aubergine.

fish sauce also called nam pla or nuoc nam; made from pulverised, salted, fermented fish, most often anchovies. Has a pungent smell and strong taste; use sparingly.

five-spice powder fragrant mixture of ground cinnamon, cloves, star anise, sichuan pepper and fennel seeds.

flour, plain all-purpose flour made from wheat.

ginger also known as green or root ginger.

juniper berries dried berries of an evergreen tree; used for their gamy flavour.

kaffir lime small yellow-green coloured, wrinkled-skinned citrus fruit.

kaffir lime leaves aromatic leaves from the kaffir lime tree.

kumara orange-fleshed sweet potato often confused with yam.

lemon grass tall, clumping, lemon-smelling and tasting, sharp-edged grass; the white lower part of each stem is chopped and used in cooking.

macadamias rich, buttery nut that is native to Australia; store in refrigerator because of high oil content.

mango chutney bottled preserve based on mango; purchase from supermarkets.

mushroom

button: small, cultivated, white mushrooms with a mild flavour.

swiss brown: light- to dark-brown mushrooms with full-bodied flavour; also known as roman or cremini. Button or cap mushrooms can be substituted.

mustard

dijon: a pale brown, distinctively flavoured, fairly mild French mustard.

seeded: also known as wholegrain. A French-style coarse-grain mustard made from crushed mustard seeds and dijon-style French mustard.

yellow seeds: also known as white mustard seeds.

onion

baby: also known as pickling onion.

green: also known as scallion or (incorrectly) shallot; an immature onion picked before the bulb has formed, having a long, bright-green edible stalk.

red: also known as spanish, red spanish or bermuda onion; a sweet-flavoured, large, purple-red onion.

spring: vegetables with small white bulbs, long green leaves and narrow green-leafed tops.

paprika ground, dried red capsicum (bell pepper), available sweet or hot.

polenta a flour-like cereal made of ground corn (maize); similar to cornmeal but finer and lighter in colour.

prosciutto salted-cured, air-dried, pressed pork; usually sold in paper-thin slices, ready to eat.

pumpkin also known as squash.

risoni rice-shaped pasta.

rocket peppery tasting salad leaf; also known as arugula, rugula and rucola.

saffron available in strands or ground form; imparts a yellow-orange colour to food once infused.

sesame oil made from roasted, crushed white sesame seeds; use as a flavouring, rather than cooking medium.

soy sauce made from fermented soy beans.

spatchcock small chicken (poussin), no more than six weeks old, weighing a maximum 500g.

star anise a dried star-shaped pod that has an astringent aniseed or licorice flavour. Available whole and ground.

sugar we used coarse, granulated table sugar, also known as crystal sugar, unless otherwise specified.

brown: an extremely soft, fine granulated sugar retaining molasses for its characteristic colour and flavour.

caster: also known as superfine or finely granulated table sugar.

tabasco brand name of an extremely fiery sauce made from vinegar, hot red peppers and salt.

tomato paste triple-concentrated tomato puree used as a flavouring.

turmeric its root is dried and ground to a rich, yellow powder; intensely pungent in taste but not hot.

yogurt unflavoured, full-fat cow-milk yogurt has been used in these recipes unless stated otherwise.

zucchini also known as courgette.

index

facts and figures

These conversions are approximate only, but the difference between an exact and the approximate conversion of various liquid and dry measures is minimal and will not affect your cooking results.

Measuring equipment

The difference between one country's measuring cups and another's is, at most, within a 2 or 3 teaspoon variance. (For the record, 1 Australian metric measuring cup holds approximately 250ml.) The most accurate way of measuring dry ingredients is to weigh them. For liquids, use a clear glass or plastic jug having metric markings.

Note: NZ, Canada, USA and UK all use 15ml tablespoons. Australian tablespoons measure 20ml.

All cup and spoon measurements are level.

How to measure

When using graduated measuring cups, shake dry ingredients loosely into the appropriate cup. Do not tap the cup on a bench or tightly pack the ingredients unless directed to do so. Level the top of measuring cups and measuring spoons with a knife. When measuring liquids, place a clear glass or plastic jug having metric markings on a flat surface to check accuracy at eye level.

Dry Measures

metric	imperial
15g	1/2oz
30g	1oz
60g	2oz
90g	3oz
125g	4oz (1/4lb)
155g	5oz
185g	6oz
220g	7oz
250g	8oz (1/2lb)
280g	9oz
315g	10oz
345g	11oz
375g	12oz (3/4lb)
410g	13oz
440g	14oz
470g	15oz
500g	16oz (1lb)
750g	24oz (1 1/2lb)
1kg	32oz (2lb)

We use large eggs having an average weight of 60g.

Liquid Measures

metric	imperial
30 ml	1 fluid oz
60 ml	2 fluid oz
100 ml	3 fluid oz
125 ml	4 fluid oz
150 ml	5 fluid oz (1/4 pint/1 gill)
190 ml	6 fluid oz
250 ml (1cup)	8 fluid oz
300 ml	10 fluid oz (1/2 pint)
500 ml	16 fluid oz
600 ml	20 fluid oz (1 pint)
1000 ml (1litre)	1 3/4 pints

Helpful Measures

metric	imperial
3mm	1/8in
6mm	1/4in
1cm	1/2in
2cm	3/4in
2.5cm	1in
6cm	2 1/2in
8cm	3in
20cm	8in
23cm	9in
25cm	10in
30cm	12in (1ft)

Oven Temperatures

These oven temperatures are only a guide. Always check the manufacturer's manual.

	°C (Celsius)	°F (Fahrenheit)	Gas Mark
Very slow	120	250	1
Slow	150	300	2
Moderately slow	160	325	3
Moderate	180 –190	350 – 375	4
Moderately hot	200 – 210	400 – 425	5
Hot	220 – 230	450 – 475	6
Very hot	240 – 250	500 – 525	7

at your fingertips

These elegant slipcovers store up to 10 mini books and make the books instantly accessible.

And the metric measuring cups and spoons make following our recipes a piece of cake.

Book Holder
Australia: $13.10 (incl. GST).
Elsewhere: $A21.95.

Metric Measuring Set
Australia: $6.50 (incl. GST).
New Zealand: $A8.00.
Elsewhere: $A9.95.
Prices include postage and handling. This offer is available in all countries.

Mail or fax Photocopy and complete the coupon below and post to ACP Books Reader Offer, ACP Publishing, GPO Box 4967, Sydney NSW 2001, or fax to (02) 9267 4967.

Phone Have your credit card details ready, then phone 136 116 (Mon-Fri, 8.00am-6.00pm; Sat, 8.00am-6.00pm).

Australian residents We accept the credit cards listed on the coupon, money orders and cheques.

Overseas residents We accept the credit cards listed on the coupon, drafts in $A drawn on an Australian bank, and also British, New Zealand and U.S. cheques in the currency of the country of issue. Credit card charges are at the exchange rate current at the time of payment.

Photocopy and complete coupon below

- -

☐ **Book Holder** ☐ **Metric Measuring Set**
Please indicate number(s) required.

Mr/Mrs/Ms _____

Address _____

_____

Postcode _____ Country _____

Ph: Business hours ( ) _____

I enclose my cheque/money order for $ _____ payable to ACP Publishing.

OR: please charge $ _____ to my ☐ Bankcard ☐ Mastercard

☐ Visa ☐ American Express ☐ Diners Club

Expiry date ____ /____

Card number

Cardholder's signature _____

Please allow up to 30 days delivery within Australia.
Allow up to 6 weeks for overseas deliveries.
Both offers expire 31/12/03. HLMR02

Food director Pamela Clark
Food editor Louise Patniotis
ACP BOOKS STAFF
Editorial director Susan Tomnay
Creative director Hieu Nguyen
Senior editor Julie Collard
Designer Mary Keep
Publishing manager (sales) Jennifer McDonald
Publishing manager (rights & new titles) Jane Hazell
Assistant brand manager Donna Gianniotis
Pre-press by Harry Palmer
Production manager Carol Currie
Publisher Sue Wannan
Group publisher Jill Baker
Chief executive officer John Alexander
Produced by ACP Books, Sydney.
Printing by Dai Nippon Printing in Hong Kong.
Published by ACP Publishing Pty Limited, 54 Park St, Sydney; GPO Box 4088, Sydney, NSW 1028. Ph: (02) 9282 8618 Fax: (02) 9267 9438.
acpbooks@acp.com.au
www.acpbooks.com.au
To order books phone 136 116.
Send recipe enquiries to Recipeenquiries@acp.com.au
Australia Distributed by Network Services, GPO Box 4088, Sydney, NSW 1028. Ph: (02) 9282 8777 Fax: (02) 9264 3278.
United Kingdom Distributed by Australian Consolidated Press (UK), Moulton Park Business Centre, Red House Road, Moulton Park, Northampton, NN3 6AQ. Ph: (01604) 497 531 Fax: (01604) 497 533 acpukltd@aol.com
Canada Distributed by Whitecap Books Ltd, 351 Lynn Ave, North Vancouver, BC, V7J 2C4, Ph: (604) 980 9852.
New Zealand Distributed by Netlink Distribution Company, Level 4, 23 Hargreaves St, College Hill, Auckland 1, Ph: (9) 302 7616.
South Africa Distributed by: PSD Promotions (Pty) Ltd, PO Box 1175, Isando 1600, SA, Ph: (011) 392 6065.

Clark, Pamela.
Roast.

Includes index.
ISBN 1 86396 277 8

1. Cookery. 2. Stoves.
I. Title: Australian Women's Weekly.
(Series: Australian Women's Weekly mini series).
641.58

Cover: Gremolata-crumbed roast leg of lamb, page 16.
Stylist Michelle Noerianto
Photographer Joe Filshie
Back cover: At left, roasted root vegetables, page 44; at right, slow-roasted veal breast with soft polenta, page 46.
Additional photography Stuart Scott
Additional styling Wendy Berecry
Home economist for additional photography Cathie Lonnie
The publishers would like to thank Empire Homewares for props used in photography.